Jokes to tell the Queen

and some important messages for her

Dedicated with great affection to
Her Majesty the Queen
"We hope we make you smile"

Bloomsbury

Contents

Introduction 1

Corgi Chuckles
and other Jokes about Animals 2

Tea Trip 14

Palatial Professors
and other School Squealers 18

Fantasy Royal Family 28

Royal Rib Ticklers
and other Family Howlers 30

Posh Palaces **40**

Noble But No Bell? **42**
and other jokes for someone who lives in a
House Without a Doorbell

Queenly Quiz **52**

What Rules Would You Make
if You Were The Queen (or King)? **60**

Thank You Everyone –
A list of people who sent in jokes **67**

At the bottom of the pages you will also
discover these:

> **?** did you know...

! **❝Important messages for the Queen❞**

INTRODUCTION

Can you imagine what it must be like to be the Queen? She's got lots more pocket money than you'll ever have, her own yacht, a special aeroplane and train to use, and she lives in a house with loads of bedrooms. Unlike you, she's got servants who will make her breakfast for her and clean out her bedroom. If she wants to go somewhere, she has a chauffeur to drive her car – and who will wash it afterwards if it gets muddy.

But, on the other hand, not only does the Queen have to rule the United Kingdom and Northern Ireland but she is also Head of the Commonwealth as well. So, wherever she goes, Elizabeth II has to speak to people, be nice to them, shake their hands, and smile all the time – even if she's got a toothache or a bunged-up nose!

Elizabeth II was crowned on 2 June 1953 – which means she's been Queen for 43 years! But, on 21 April 1996, she will be celebrating her seventieth birthday, which is why, after thinking about all the hard work the Queen has to do, we thought we'd put together all of your favourite jokes which you told us you would like to tell the Queen when you get to meet her. After all, everyone needs a laugh to make them happy. So why not open up and celebrate with the Queen and with a chuckle?

Dear Queen,
If you are reading this
— HAPPY BIRTHDAY FROM
ALL OF US!
(Especially those mentioned
on page 67!)

CORGI CHUCKLES
and other jokes about animals

*E*veryone knows that the Queen loves animals – she keeps corgis and labradors and has lots of horses, some of which are race horses. So these jokes will be guaranteed to have the Queen and her corgis chuckling.

Why do French people
eat snails?
Because they don't like fast food.

Why couldn't Batman
go fishing?
Because Robin had eaten all the
worms.

*What's round and furry and smells
of mint?
A polo bear.*

What's round, made of chocolate, and sits on the sea
bed?
An oyster egg.

The Queen once had a parrot and if she pulled his
right leg he said prayers. If she pulled his left leg he
said Grace. One day, a priest came along and said
"I wonder what would happen if I pulled both legs?"
The parrot replied, "I'd fall off my perch, idiot!"

Why do goats wear bells?
Because their horns don't work.

**What do you call a deer with no eyes?
No eye deer ...**

What's black and white and red all over?
A sunburnt penguin.

"I know where the treasure is hidden!"
Hugh Haywood, 6, Widcombe Infant School, Bath

When do elephants paint their toe-nails red?
When they want to hide in the cherry tree.

What's the difference between a piano and a fish?
You can't tuna fish!

What did the baby hen say to his father?
Look what marmalade.

What do you call married horses?
A bridle and groom.

How many "f"s in this: A farmer found a
fox in a field?
None. There are no "f"s in "this".

What pet does the Queen keep in her
loo?
The privy seal.

What do you get if you cross a royal dog
with a plumber?
A corgi contractor.

What goes oom oom?
A cow walking backwards.

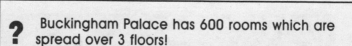

Where do you go if you need a pat
on the head?
Under a cow.

How do you stop the corgi from barking in the back
garden?
Put him in the front garden.

? Buckingham Palace has 600 rooms which are
spread over 3 floors!

How do you know if there has been an elephant in the fridge?
By the footprints in the butter.

Why does Mr Blobby's dog have a shiny nose?
Because he takes his Blob Martins every day.

Why did the fish blush?
Because it saw the Queen Elizabeth's bottom.

What's the best thing to do if your corgi swallows a dictionary?
Take the words right out of his mouth.

A horse walks into a shop and the shopkeeper says, "What's with the long face?"

What do you get if you cross a cow with a camel?
A lumpy milkshake.

What do corgis do in cold weather?
Sit around the fire.

What do corgis do in very cold weather?
Light the fire.

What would happen if the Queen had a cow, a duck and a goat?
She'd have cream quackers and cheese every day for breakfast.

> **!** "Please give the pensioners more money because they have worked for a long time. They shouldn't have to worry about keeping warm in winter."
> Victoria Catherine Darce, 10, Seascale School, Cumbria

Why did the one-eyed bird cross the road?
To get to the bird's eye shop.

How do you hire a horse?
Put it on four bricks.

What does a man do standing up, a lady sitting down and a corgi on 3 legs?
Shake hands.

What do you get if you cross a sheep with a kangaroo?
A woolly jumper.

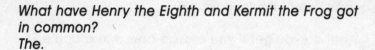

What have Henry the Eighth and Kermit the Frog got in common?
The.

What goes 99-bonk?
A centipede with a wooden leg.

Why couldn't the two elephants go swimming?
Because they had only one pair of trunks.

What's the difference between a dog and a flea?
A dog can have fleas but a flea can't have dogs.

Why do elephants have big ears?
Because Noddy won't pay the ransom.

? Buckingham Palace wasn't used as a royal palace until 1837 and wasn't called Buckingham Palace until 1843.

What do birds eat for breakfast?
Tweetabix.

What did the dog say when it sat on the sandpaper?
Ruff, ruff!

Why didn't the hedgehog wash his hair?
Because he'd left his head and shoulders on the motor way.

What is black and white and noisy?
A penguin playing the drums.

What do you call a dog on a warm day?
A hot dog.

What do you call a short-sighted dinosaur?
I don't think he saw us. (Say it fast.)

Why aren't there any tablets in the jungle?
Because the parrots-eat-em-all.

Why did the elephant cross the road twice?
Because it was a double-crosser.

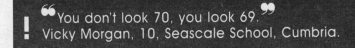

What kind of computer system do animals play in the jungle?
Mortal wombat.

Which American city has lots of cows?
Moo York.

Why did the hedgehog say "ouch"?
Because his prickles were inside out.

What do you call a badger with a red bottom?
A badger with nappy rash.

What is a cow's favourite game?
Moosical chairs.

What do you call a fish with a fishing rod?
A fishing fish.

How do pigs dress?
In mud.

What do you say if you pass a cat with a log?
A catalogue!

Why did the dinosaur have spots?
Because it had chicken pox.

What goes up slowly and comes down fast?
An elephant in a lift.

? Buckingham Palace was originally called Arlington House and was built in 1674. It wasn't until 1703 that it became known as Buckingham House. In 1761, the house was sold to George III for £28,000 and it then became the property of the Crown.

What do you call an elephant that can't do sums?
Dumbo.

What animals in Noah's Ark didn't come in pairs?
Worms, they came in apples.

Why do bees fly with their legs crossed?
Because they are looking for the BP station.

Why is a turkey like a cushion?
Because they are both full of stuffing.

What do you get if you cross a snowman with a
man-eating shark?
Frostbites.

What do you call a stag with no eyes?
Still no idea!

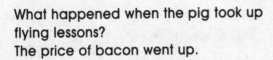

What happened when the pig took up
flying lessons?
The price of bacon went up.

What goes to bed with its shoes on?
A horse.

Why did one snake ask the other snake if it was
poisonous?
It bit him!

Why did the hedgehog cross the road?
To see his flat mate.

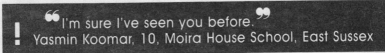

Which fly makes films?
Stephen Speilbug.

What did the Pink Panther say when he stood on an ant?
Dead, ant, dead ant, dead ant dead ant dead ant dead ant dead ant dead ant … (sing it to the tune!).

Why do frogs hop?
Because they don't want the French to get their legs.

Ten cats were on a boat, one cat jumped off. How many cats were left?
None — the others were copy cats.

Why did the punk cross the road?
Because he was stapled to the chicken.

Why do bees hum?
Because they don't know the words.

What do cows drink?
Mooshakes.

What do you get if you cross a tiger and a sheep?
A stripey woolly.

Why did the tortoise cross the road?
Because he wanted to get to the Shell Station.

What do you get if you cross a hare and a cow?
A hairy cow.

What did the dinosaur say to the elephant?
Nothing. They can't talk.

What did the grape do when the elephant sat on it?
Gave a little whine.

Why did the lobster blush?
Because he got stuck in the seaweed.

How do you keep flies out of the kitchen?
Put all the rubbish in the living room.

What's the best way to stop fish smelling?
Cut off their noses.

What's the difference between
Indian and African elephants?
About 3,000 miles.

How do you weigh a whale?
At a whale weight station.

Why did the cow laugh when he slipped on the ice?
Because it was no use crying over spilt milk.

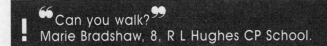

! “Can you walk?”
  Marie Bradshaw, 8, R L Hughes CP School.

11

What's a slug?
A snail with a housing problem.

Why did the chicken jump off a bridge?
Because he was sick of crossing the road.

What do you give a sick pig.
Oinkment.

Where do you send a sick wasp?
Waspital.

Why did the cow cross the road?
Because it was the chicken's day off.

Why did the dinosaur cross the forest?
Because roads weren't invented then!

How does an octopus go into battle?
Well armed.

What is a ewe's favourite doll?
Barrrrbie.

Why did the chewing gum cross the road?
It got stuck on the chicken's foot!

What animals need oiling?
Mice — because they squeak.

Why do tigers eat raw meat?
Because they don't know how to cook.

Why do birds fly south in winter?
Because it's too far to walk.

? The Queen has her own football club called the
Royal Household Football Club!

Why does a lion wear a furry coat?
Because he'd look stupid in a plastic raincoat.

What's worse than a giraffe with a sore throat?
A centipede with blisters.

How do you know if carrots are good for your eyesight?
Have you ever seen a rabbit wearing glasses?

What do you do if there is a gorilla in your bed?
Sleep somewhere else!

Why did the pig cross the road?
To get to the piggybank.

How do you spell "hungry horse" in four letters?
MTGG.

Who is the Queen of hares and rabbits?
Hare Majesty.

What goes tick, tick, woof, woof?
A watchdog.

How do you communicate with a fish?
Drop it a line.

Where does a horse go when it's ill?
Horsepital.

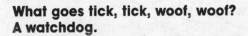

What's black and white and runs on sixteen wheels?
A zebra on roller skates.

TEA TRIP

If you invited the Queen to tea and she wrote back saying she was coming, have you any idea what you'd give her to eat? Would it be Coronation Chicken washed down with Queen Anne tea? Or Palatial Plaice followed by Royal Trifle or Queen of Puddings?

*M*y Royal Tea Menu would be:

*T*his is what I would talk to the Queen about:

*T*he other guests at tea would be:

ROYAL TEA ETIQUETTE

1 You should send your invitation to "The Private Secretary to Her Majesty the Queen, Buckingham Palace, London".

2 When the Queen arrives at your house, wait until she offers you her hand before you shake it.

3 Curtsey or bow when you say "Good afternoon, Your Majesty".

4 Introduce your granny to the Queen by saying "Granny, may I introduce you to Her Majesty the Queen?".

5 When the Queen speaks to you the first time, reply and call her "Your Majesty". After that, you can call her "Ma'am" (say it like "marm").

6 You'll need to lay a space at the table for either the Queen's Lady in Waiting or her Private Secretary and also the police officer who will accompany the Queen to protect her.

7 The Queen will be the guest of honour so make sure she has the best seat.

8 None of your guests should leave until the Queen has gone home.

Practical Tips

Practical Tip Number 1: HOW TO HOLD A HANDBAG

Never use a bag with a shoulder strap — with all that
hand shaking it will keep on sliding down your arm
every time it gets wobbled up and down. Instead,
you need a large bag with small handles. Holding it
is easy: just hook the handles over the wrist of the
hand that you won't be using for handshaking and
then draw your elbow into your wrist like this:

Do your best to hold the bag like this all day. (The
Queen has to, so why shouldn't you!)

PALATIAL PROFESSORS
and other school squealers

*Even though the Queen
wasn't sent to school herself, she had to work hard
with her private tutor at home.
So she probably worked even harder than the
biggest swot in your school because the teacher was
never distracted by anyone else.
We reckon the Queen deserves a good laugh!*

TEACHER: What nuts can you hang pictures on, JIMMY?
JIMMY: Walnuts.

TEACHER: Sarah, what has a head and a tail but no body?
SARAH: A penny, miss.

TEACHER: If I laid two eggs on one side of the table and two on the other, how many would I have?
PUPIL: I don't know, sir, but I bet you couldn't do it.

TEACHER: If I had four apples in one hand and five oranges in the other, what would I have?
PUPIL: Big hands, miss!

TEACHER: Where does the Queen keep her armies?
TRACEY: Up her sleevies, sir.

TEACHER: What do Italians play at parties?
JODIE: Pasta parcel.

TEACHER: What do you call a woman covered in yellow grease?
HANNAH: Marge!

TEACHER: What do you call a man with a spade on his head?
JOSH: Doug, miss.

TEACHER: Where is Hadrian's Wall?
CINDY: Around Hadrian's house, miss.

TEACHER: Why does the word "young lady" need a "Y"?
MICHAEL: Because if it didn't have one it would be a young lad!

TEACHER: Why does the Queen employ Beefeaters?
ANNA: Because she likes their burgers.

PUPIL: Miss, what's white when dirty and black when clean?
TEACHER: A blackboard.

TEACHER: John, what do you call a man with a plank on his head?
JOHN: Edwood.

TEACHER: Why did the clown wear a red nose?
VICTOR: To make him look funny, miss.

TEACHER: What's the difference between a ball and a Prince?
ADAM: One is thrown in the air and the other is heir to the throne.

TEACHER: What can be found all over the house?
JACK: A roof sir?

TEACHER: What does the Queen use when she gets a puncture?
LAURA: A Union Jack!

? The Queen receives over 100,000 letters every year — so many that Buckingham Palace has to have its own Post Office.

TEACHER: Where does the Queen come from?
JOEL: Alaska.
TEACHER: No, don't bother. I'll ask her myself when I next see her.

TEACHER: What's the worst thing to find in a second-hand shop?
DOUGLAS: A toilet roll.

TEACHER: What runs around Buckingham Palace but can't move?
THOMAS: The perimeter wall.

TEACHER: How do you make a band stand?
YASMINE: Take away their chairs, sir.

TEACHER: Why did the bald man go for a walk?
REBECCA: To get some fresh hair.

TEACHER: Where does the Queen play tennis, Sarah?
SARAH: On the crown court.

TEACHER: Which are the poshest ski resorts?
ALYS: The ones covered with Royal icing.

TEACHER: What does the Queen drink?
ALISON: Royal tea.

TEACHER: What was the first thing Queen Elizabeth did when she came to the throne?
PHILIP: Sit on it.

! 66 Happy Birthday, you are still younger than my granny. 99
Alys Randall, 7^1/$_2$, Evenlode Primary School, Penarth

TEACHER: Which hand does the Queen use to stir her tea?

OWEN: She doesn't — she uses her spoon like everyone else!

TEACHER: What's the difference between the Queen and a storm?
THOMAS: The Queen reigns longer.

MORGAN: Mrs Jones, do you notice any change in me?
MRS JONES: Why?
MORGAN: I've just swallowed my bus fare.

MRS WHITFIELD: What kind of cheese is made backwards?
TIMOTHY: Edam, miss.

MRS PENRY-WILLIAMS: Nick and Jess, which one of the Queen's relatives invented the fire place?
NICK AND JESS: Alfred the Great!

MR BIRCHALL: What's the sport of Queens?
HANNAH: Windsor-fing.

MR HARLE: Miriam, how many letters are there in the alphabet?
MIRIAM: 24 sir.
MR HARLE: Why?
MIRIAM: Because I have a letter saying I have to miss PE.

? The Queen owns the postal system which is why it is called the Royal Mail. Consequently, all the letters sent by the Queen don't need a stamp. Instead they are franked with EIIR.

MR ROBERTS-WRAY: Why wouldn't the Queen make a good teacher?
ADAM: Because she doesn't know all her subjects.

MRS BURROWS: How do you make a sausage roll.
SCARLET: Push it down the hill.

TEACHER: Who invented fire?
ASHLEY: Oh, some bright spark.

MRS ASHWORTH: Why did the Queen throw the clock out of the window?
JESSICA: To see time fly.

MRS COOK: What does the Queen keep bottles closed with?
CHLOE: Corkies, Miss.

MRS LAMBE: Why did the Queen say ouchhh when she walked into the bar?
JAMIE: Because it was a metal bar!

TEACHER: Who was the father of the Black Prince?
SAM: Old King Cole.

TEACHER: Why does the Queen wave her right hand?
SALLY: Because the left one's mine!

TEACHER: Why did the Queen bring a hammer to school?
DANIELLE: Because they were breaking up.

MRS REAST: Lucy, you missed school yesterday, didn't you?
LUCY: No miss, I didn't miss it one bit!

MRS SANDERS: Why did the policeman get run over?
LEE: Because he wasn't looking.

TEACHER: Why did the robber have a bath?
CHRISTPHER: Because he wanted to make a clean getaway.

MRS BUXTON: How do you start a teddy bear race?
AMY: Ready, teddy, go!

TEACHER: What's 300 metres high and wobbles?
SHAUN: The Trifle Tower, miss.

TEACHER: What's frozen water?
DAWN: Ice.
TEACHER: What's frozen tea?
DAWN: Iced tea.
TEACHER: What's frozen cream?
DAWN: Ice cream.
TEACHER: What's frozen ink?
DAWN: Iced ink.
TEACHER: Well, have a bath then!

> **?** You can't sue the Queen or take her to court — because the court belongs to the Queen!

TEACHER: What do you call a lady with two lavatories?
RYAN: Lulu, sir?

TEACHER: What goes "Now you see me, now you don't, now you see me, now you don't"?
NATASHA: A snowman on a zebra crossing!

TEACHER: What goes up but never comes down?
KIRSTY: Your age, sir.

TEACHER: How can you cut the sea?
SANDEEP: With a seasaw.

MISS SUMNER: What month has 28 days?
JACK: All of them miss!

PUPIL: Miss, should you write with your left hand or right hand?
TEACHER: Neither, you should write with a pen.

MISS REEVES: What is the difference between a fireman and a soldier?
ALISON: Well, you can't dip a fireman in your egg.

TEACHER: Why are goldfish orange?
MICHELLE: Because the water makes them rusty.

What did the cross-eyed teacher say?
"I can't control my pupils!"

MISS WALTER: What flies and wobbles?
GRANT: A jellycopter.

MRS GIBSON: How do you stay cool at a
football match?
STUART: Stand next to a fan.

TEACHER: What do you call a man with
eight balaclavas on his head?
RHYS: Anything you like — he won't hear
you!

**TEACHER: What happened to the plant
in the maths lesson?**
GEMMA: It grew square roots.

TEACHER: In which battle did Nelson die?
JACK: His last one, miss.

 Buckingham Palace has over 300 telephones!

Practical Tips

Practical Tip Number 2: WHAT TO KEEP IN YOUR HANDBAG

Exactly what the Queen keeps in her own handbag is a secret, but the following items would probably come in useful to her:

A handkerchief (for blowing Royal noses)

A lipstick in "Balmoral Red" (for covering up what has been worn away with all that talking to people)

A list of things you have to do (so that you don't forget who you are meant to visit next)

A Walkman (so that you won't get bored on the journey home)

A torch (in case the lights go out)

A packet of sweeties (to stop you getting hungry)

A plastic bag (to put all your leftover food in so that you can take it home to the Corgis)

A pair of gloves (in case all the people you have to shake hands with have got sticky hands)

A notebook (so that you can write down what you're going to get everyone for Christmas)

A pencil or pen (to do all your writing with)

Can you think of anything else which you would find useful?

FANTASY ROYAL FAMILY

Everyone, at some stage, has tried to imagine what it must be like to be the Queen. But, can you begin to imagine what it would be like if your family was actually the Royal Family? Do you think they'd be any good at it? Would your Dad make a better Prince of Wales, do you think, than a Duke of Edinburgh? Would your auntie be better as the Queen Mother than your Granny? Why not have some fun matching your own family to the Royal one and create your very own Fantasy Royal Family?

REAL ROYAL	FANTASY ROYAL FAMILY

THE QUEEN ---

THE DUKE OF EDINBURGH ------------------------

THE QUEEN MOTHER ---------------------------

THE PRINCE OF WALES ---------------------------

THE PRINCESS OF WALES -------------------------

THE PRINCESS ROYAL ---------------------------

THE DUKE OF YORK -----------------------------

PRINCE EDWARD ------------------------------

THE CORGIS -----------------------------------

ROYAL RIB-TICKLERS
and other family howlers

The Queen has a very large family and invites them to stay with her as often as possible. Don't you think she deserves to get her own back on them by telling some of these jokes?

Why did the hand cross the road?
To get to the second-hand shop.

What do sea monsters like to eat?
Fish and ships.

What is red and stupid?
A blood clot.

What happened to the man who always wore sunglasses?
He took a very dim view of things.

What's the last thing you take off before going to bed?
Your feet — off the floor.

Why do eskimos eat candles?
For light refreshment.

When does a bed change size?
At night — when two feet are added.

What did the traffic lights say to the sports car?
Don't look now, I'm changing.

**Why didn't the skeleton go to the party?
Because it had nobody to go with.**

Why didn't the milkman get an OBE?
Because he lost his bottle.

QUEEN: Arise Sir Gavin, you are now a Knight.
SIR GAVIN: Can I have a moon to go with the night? I'm afraid of the dark.

What did the referee say to the pushy snooker player?
"Go to the back of the cue!"

*DOCTOR, DOCTOR — I THINK I'M A GOAT!
How long has this been going on?
SINCE I WAS A KID.*

Did you hear about the fight in the biscuit tin? A bandit hit the penguin with a club and tied him up with a blue ribbon. He got away in a taxi eating a sandwich.

Did you hear about the tap dancer? She broke her leg when she fell in the sink.

? When the telephone operator at Buckingham Palace has to connect the Queen to the Queen Mother, she has to say: "Your Majesty? Her Majesty, Your Majesty".

Why did the orange cross the road? Because he wanted to be orange squash.

What's yellow and goes up and down?
A banana in a lift.

What did the big chimney say to the little chimney?
You're too young to smoke.

What do you say if a biscuit gets run over?
Crumbs!

What's green and hairy and goes up and down?
A gooseberry in a lift.

DOCTOR: Did you drink a glass of orange juice after your bath?
PATIENT: No — After drinking the bath I didn't fancy the orange juice.

What did the big candle say to the little candle?
I'm going out tonight.

What did the Queen say on the 1st January?
Happy New Year!

What's the Queen's favourite game?
A game of chess — because she knows all the moves.

> **"**If we laughed a lot we would get along better.**"**
> Jack Buckner, 9, Pinner Park Middle School

What do skeletons eat off?
Bone china plates.

What did the Queen's astronauts see in
their kitchen?
Unidentified frying objects.

Two tomatoes are on a plate, which one is the
cowboy?
Neither — they are both red skins.

BOYS: Can you pull a rabbit out of your hat?
MAGICIAN: No — I washed my hare last
night and I can't do a thing with it.

**Why does the Queen wave her hand?
Because if she nodded her head her
crown would fall off.**

What would you do if you met a cannibal?
Give him a hand.

MAN IN BUS QUEUE: How long will the next bus be?
INSPECTOR: About 11 metres, same as the rest.

Why did the skeleton cross the road?
To get to the Body Shop.

What is big and ugly and covered with spots?
A monster with chicken pox.

"Polly — put the kettle on!"
"No — I don't think it would suit me."

? The Royal Family has so much gold, silver and
crockery that there is The Yeoman of the Gold and
Silver Pantry and The Yeoman of the Glass and China!

What did the salad say to the fridge?
Close that door — I'm dressing.

What does a policeman have for dinner?
Truncheonmeat.

What's green and goes camping?
A boy sprout.

*Why didn't the Queen cross the potato
patch?*
She was afraid the eyes would look up her skirt.

What happens if you put Mr Blobby in the bath for
too long?
He gets a crinkly bottom.

DOCTOR, DOCTOR — I FEEL LIKE A PAIR OF
CURTAINS!
Oh shut up and pull yourself together!

Why was the Pharoah confused?
Because his daddy was a mummy.

What did the Queen's policeman say to
his tummy?
You're under a vest.

Why did the Queen sit on the clock?
Because she wanted to be on time for her party.

Why is the sea always restless?
Because it's got so many rocks in its bed.

" Do you like travelling around the world? **"**
Kerri Denman, 10, Sandcross School, Surrey

What did one eye say to the other eye?
Something between us smells.

Why did the Weeping Willow weep?
Because it saw the Pine Tree pine.

Why do you need an umbrella when you see the Queen?
Because wherever she goes she's always reigning.

What can the Queen say without saying anything?
Anything but ANYTHING.

Why did the golfer have four shoes?
In case there was a hole in one.

Why does the Queen never race?
Because she is Queen Elizabeth the Second.

What does the Queen eat at birthday parties?
Royal Jelly.

What do two oceans say when they meet?
Nothing. They just wave!

"Waiter, waiter — this soup tastes funny."
"Why aren't you laughing then?"

What is a net?
Holes tied together with string.

> **?** Royal Footmen are trained for 3 years and are given a certificate on completion of their training.

What do you call a girl with a frog on her head?
Lily.

How do you flatten a ghost?
With a spirit level.

What does the robot's tombstone say?
Rust in peace.

DOCTOR, DOCTOR — I FEEL LIKE A CRICKET
BALL!
How's that?
DON'T YOU START!

Where does the Queen keep her knight's armour?
On her knights!

What do you call Postman Pat when
he's sacked?
Pat.

What did the biscuits say top the almonds?
You're nuts and we're crackers.

Why did the tomato blush?
Because it saw the salad dressing.

Where does the vampire keep his money?
At the blood bank.

The Queen bought a new coat. It fitted like a glove — after all, it had five sleeves.

What did the Queen Mother say when she had her hip replaced?
Hip hip hooray!

What do you get if you cross a skunk with a boomerang?
A smell that's hard to get rid of.

What do you call two robbers?
A pair of knickers.

If an earl is made an OBE, does he become an Earlobe?

Why did the skeleton run up the tree?
Because the dog was after his bones.

The Queen's corgi went into a shop and went "Bang! Bang! Bang!" on the counter with his paws and said "Can I have some Bonios please?"

The shopkeeper gave him some Bonios and off he went to the Palace.

The next day he went to the shop again and went "Bang! Bang! Bang!" on the counter and asked for some more Bonios. The shopkeeper said "Hey, stop that racket, otherwise I'll nail your paws to the counter".

Practical Tips

Practical Tip Number 3: **HOW TO WAVE**

This is easy — but only if you have to do it for a short while. Bending your elbow, raise your hand up towards your face. Now, still keeping your elbow in at your waist, waggle your hand up and down. Don't forget to keep smiling at the same time!

(NB This waving is most often done whilst sitting in the back of a car and looking out of a window.)

Practical Tip Number 4: **TAKING A CORGI FOR A WALK**

1 Find a corgi.

2 Attach a lead to the corgi's collar.

3 Put on a headscarf, an anorak and green wellies (see Practical Tip Number 6 for help with this).

4 Walk around your garden with the corgi.

5 Return to the house and give the corgi some food.
6 Remove your headscarf, anorak and wellies.

7 Sit down to watch Coronation Street.

POSH PALACES

Buckingham Palace has been around for over 300 years and has got lots of draughty rooms (about 600 of them!) and corridors. If you were the Queen or King you'd quite possibly find that you'd want to make a number of home improvements and do some D.I.Y. (if you only had the time) to make everything cosier. Imagine, though, if you had the chance to design a Royal palace from scratch. What special features would you put in? How many bedrooms would you want? Would you want your own private cinema?

Or perhaps you'd have a heated indoor swimming pool? Would you have escalators so you wouldn't have to climb the stairs? Or solar-powered central heating to save on the earth's resources?

We've given you lots of space at the end of the book to design your very own palace. Remember, you'll need to do a floor plan for each of the floors in your palace and it would be best if you named each of the rooms as you go.

NOBLE BUT NO BELL?
and other jokes for someone who lives in a house without a doorbell

*B*ecause the Queen always arrives home in a car or a coach she doesn't even carry a house key. And no one knocks on her door — they always use the side entrances. But the Queen is bound to appreciate a good Knock, Knock joke when she comes across it!

Knock, knock!
Who's there?
Isabel.
Isabel who?
Isabel necessary on a bike?

Knock, knock!
Who's there?
Doctor.
Doctor who?
Do me a favour and clear off.

Knock, knock!
Who's there?
Policeman.
Policeman who?
Policeman Creaseman.

Knock, knock!
Who's there?
Smartie Pants.
Smartie Pants who?
You've got a smartie in your pants.

Knock, knock!
Who's there?
Heave.
Heave who?
Heave who my hearties.

> **❝**Please can you try to stop the nuclear testing in the South Pacific. It is killing the fish and not doing any good to the environment.**❞**
> Jonathan Delchar, 10, Sandcross School, Surrey

Knock, knock!
Who's there?
Lettuce.
Lettuce who?
Lettuce in and you'll find out.

Knock, knock!
Who's there?
Pencil.
Pencil who?
Pencil Sharpener.

Knock, knock!
Who's there?
Nanna.
Nanna who?
Nanna your business!

Knock, knock!
Who's there?
Inspector.
Inspector who?
Inspector Gadget.

Knock, knock!
Who's there?
Cows go.
Cows go who?
No! Cows go moo!

Knock, knock!
Who's there?
Lettuce.
Lettuce who?
Lettuce in I'm hungry!

? No one waits on the Queen at breakfast — she serves herself in her private dining room.

Knock, knock!
Who's there?
Pudding.
Pudding who?
Pudding on your hat when it is raining is
a good idea.

Knock, knock!
Who's there?
Spook.
Spook who?
Spooketti Bolognese.

Knock, knock!
Who's there?
Santa.
Santa who?
Santa Claus. Let me in it's freezing out here.

Knock, knock!
Who's there?
Police.
Police who?
I'm just a policeman. Now open the door
or I'll have to knock the door down.

Knock, knock!
Who's there.
Purr.
Purr who?
Purrhaps I could come in to your party?

> **"**Could you spend some of your birthday money on
> the Third World?**"**
> John Martyn Bullen, 11, Sandcross School, Surrey

Knock, knock!
Who's there?
Boo.
Boo who?
Now, there's no need to cry.

Knock, knock!
Who's there?
David.
David who?
David the doorbell so I had to knock.

Knock, knock!
Who's there?
Night.
Night who?
Good night to you too!

Knock, knock!
Who's there?
You.
You who?
Yes — what do you want?

Knock, knock!
Who's there?
Hatch.
Hatch who?
Bless you!

? One of the Queen's favourite ice-creams is
chocolate mint chip.

Knock, knock!

Who's there?

Granny.

Granny who?

Knock, knock!

Who's there?

Granny.

Granny who?

Knock, knock!

Who's there?

Granny.

Granny WHO?

Knock, knock!

Who's there?

Aunty.

Aunty who?

Aunty glad granny's gone now?

Knock, knock!
Who's there?
Irish Stew.
Irish Stew who?
Irish Stew in the name of the law!

Knock, knock!
Who's there?
The Queen.
The Queen who?
The Queen who is 70.

Knock, knock!
Who's there?
Ablive.
Ablive who?
Ablive in Father Christmas.

Knock, knock!
Who's there?
Handsome.
Handsome who?
Handsome keys through the letterbox or let me in!

Knock, Knock!
Who's there?
Banana.
Banana Who?
Banana stew!

? In the days when lions and leopards were kept at the Tower of London, there used to be a Keeper of the Lions.

Knock, Knock!

Who's there?

Will you remember me tomorrow?

Yes!

Knock, Knock!

Who's there?

Will you remember me next week?

Yes!

Knock, Knock!

Who's there?

You said you'd remember me!

Knock, Knock!
Who's there?
Apple.
Apple who?
Apple stew!

Knock, Knock!
Who's there?
Kanga?
Kanga who?
No! Kangaroo!

> **"**If you ever need anyone to take your corgis for a walk, just give me a call.**"**
> ! Rebecca Thewlls, 12, Almondbury High School, Huddersfield

49

Knock, Knock!
Who's there?
Orange.
Orange who?
Orange you glad I didn't ring the bell?

Knock, Knock!
Who's there?
Banana.
Banana who?
Knock, Knock!
Who's there?
Banana.
Banana who?
Knock, Knock!
Who's there?
Orange.
Orange who?
Orange you glad I didn't say banana?

Knock, knock!
Who's there?
Scott.
Scott who?
Scott nothing to do with you.

? The Queen never went to school! She had lessons at
home instead with her sister, Princess Margaret, instead

Practical Tips

Practical Tip Number 5: HOW TO WEAR A CROWN WITHOUT IT FALLING OFF

This requires practice and it is worth watching the Queen doing it on any videos or television programmes which show the Queen at the State Opening of Parliament, to pick up some tips.

You'll need to stand in front of a mirror and then carefully place your crown on top of your head. (If you can't borrow a crown from someone, you could try making one out of cardboard or you could see if anyone has got one left over from their Christmas cracker. Alternatively, you could place a large hardback library book on your head — after all, the real Crown weighs 1.5 kg!)

Now walk slowly and regally around the room, remembering to look up at all times so that your Crown doesn't slip. Once you can do this, try waving and shaking someone's hand whilst you are wearing your Crown (see Practical Tip Number 3 for help).

QUEENLY QUIZ
(OR KINGLY KLUES)

How do you think you'd survive as the monarch? Try answering this quiz to test your regal resources. Keep a note of your score so that you can see how you did at the end.

1 YOU ARE DUE TO ATTEND A ROYAL VISIT IN AN OPEN-TOPPED HORSE-DRAWN COACH. THE PROBLEM IS IT IS NOW RAINING.
Do you:

A Cancel the trip and stay at home to watch a video.

B Put on a rainhat and macintosh and go anyway.

C Arrange to go on the visit in a car instead.

2 IT'S TIME TO REVIEW THE ROYAL FINANCES.
Do you:

A Ask Parliament to give you a raise but not give one to anyone else, and get the the Palace decorated.

B Ask for more money for all your staff.

C Say that times are hard and that everyone, including yourself, can cope without any extra cash this year.

! "Yorkie bars now cost 29p"
Rory Cahill, 10, Westgarth Primary School, Cleveland

3 YOU'RE PLANNING YOUR DIARY FOR NEXT MONTH AND HAVE TO CHOOSE BETWEEN A TRIP TO AN OLD PEOPLE'S HOME, A PREVIEW OF A FILM AND OPENING A NEW SCHOOL.
Do you:

A Decide to go to the film and say you'll try and fit the rest in some other time.

B Arrange to visit the school in the morning, the old people's home in the afternoon and the film preview in the evening.

C Say you'll go to the school and the home but ask if they can send you a video of the film to watch at home on your own.

---

4 YOU NEED TO ORDER A NEW SET OF FORMAL ROBES.
Do you:

A Pop out to the local department store and buy something off the peg.
B Arrange for a national competition to design and make the robes giving student designers a chance to make their name.
C Go to your usual dress designer for their expert advice.

? Did you know that the Queen has a Racing Pigeon Manager? He looks after her team of racing pigeons which are kept in Norfolk.

5 IT'S TIME TO RECORD YOUR ANNUAL CHRISTMAS BROADCAST.
Do you:

A Invite the film crew (who have come to record the broadcast) to have tea in the staff canteen.

B Stay around to have tea and mince pies with them.

C Offer them a special tea but have tea on your own in your private rooms.

FOR THE ANSWERS SEE NEXT PAGE...

QUIZ ANSWERS...

IF YOU ANSWERED MOSTLY 'A's:

We don't think you'd last very long in charge. You're too selfish to look after anyone but yourself. In fact, monarchs like you ended up in the Tower of London not that long ago. We suggest you abdicate.

IF YOU ANSWERED MOSTLY 'B's:

It sounds like you're made of the right stuff to survive as ruler: you make everyone equally important and are prepared to put in a hard day's work. Your crown certainly won't slip.

IF YOU ANSWERED MOSTLY 'C's:

You are usually on the right track but occasionally you obviously get tempted to think about your own comforts first. A few years more experience will teach you all you need to know.

Practical Tips

Practical Tip Number 6: WEARING A HEADSCARF, ANORAK AND GREEN WELLIES

This outfit is essential for outings to the country and for corgi walking (see Practical Tip Number 4).

First the headscarf

Fold it like this:

Then tie it around your head like this:

Then tie a knot in the scarf under your chin. (This is known as a Knightsbridge Knot.)

Second the anorak

This should preferably be in navy blue or dark green although an old skiing jacket would do. Make sure the poppers are done up at all times, It is best to wear an anorak with your hands in your pockets.

Lastly the wellies

These must be green but should never be bright green. At a pinch, you could get away with black ones.

Practical Tip Number 7: TALKING TO STRANGERS

The ability to do this is really successfully can only be acquired with years of practice (after all the Queen's been doing it for seventy years!). But here are some handy phrases which might help you to get by:

"Hello!"

"Oh really?"

"How very interesting!"

"Gosh — did you make it yourself?"

"So nice to have met you."

"Thank you for coming."

"Goodbye!"

Practical Tip Number 8: STOPPING YOUR FEET FROM ACHING ON WALKABOUTS

1 Never wear high heels.

2 Always make sure your shoes fit properly.

3 Wear socks, not bare feet, on hot days.

4 Avoid getting chilblains!

5 Always make sure your feet are clean and smell sweet!

6 Sit down every now and then.

WHAT RULES WOULD YOU MAKE IF YOU WERE THE QUEEN (OR KING)?

If it was up to you, what special benefits would you make sure children had? Would you declare that everyone was given a free bag of sweets on days that have the letter "d" in them? Or would you say that no one had to go to school on days when they have to do maths? Now's your chance to write down your own List of Rules of your Kingdom.

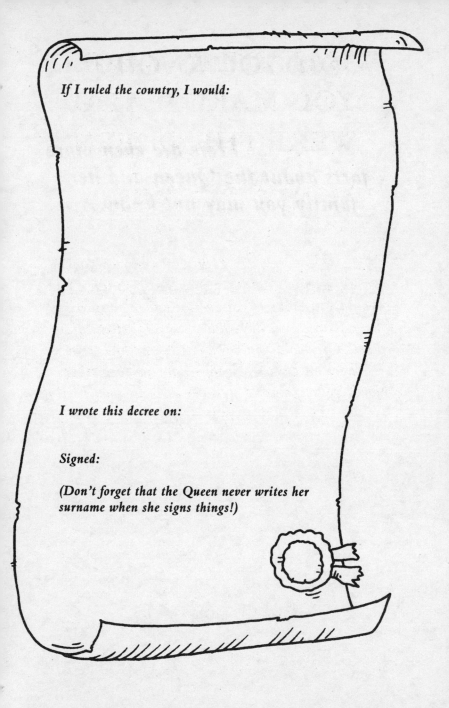

If I ruled the country, I would:

I wrote this decree on:

Signed:

(Don't forget that the Queen never writes her surname when she signs things!)

DID YOU KNOW?

Here are even more facts about the Queen and her family you may not know...

? When the Queen goes to bed, an armed policeman stands guard outside her bedroom throughout the night.

? The Queen keeps a copy of her day's itinerary in her handbag which she refers to throughout the day.

? The Keeper of the Privy Purse is the man in charge of the royal housekeeping money.

? The Queen never carries any money — so what does she keep in her handbag?

? The Queen only wears a crown at her own Coronation and at the State Opening of Parliament. It weighs 1.5 kg, has 2,783 diamonds, 277 pearls, 18 sapphires, 11 emeralds and 5 rubies. The largest diamond in the crown has 309 carats and is called the Second Star of Africa.

? The Crown Jewels actually consist of 58 pieces!

? The Royal Train is bombproof.

? When the Queen presides over the State Opening of Parliament, she wears a dress which has a velvet train which is nearly 5.5 metres long!

? Royal invitations are actually commands and should never be declined. If you get invited to tea with the Queen, you should reply "I have the honour to obey Her Majesty's command".

? The Queen's handbags are made by a British company based in Surrey called S. Launer and Company.

? The Queen's corgis eat Pedigree Chum and Spratt's dog biscuits.

? For her coronation, the Queen had a special lipstick created for her called "Balmoral Red".

? The Queen's shoes are made by H and M Rayne Limited.

? Coronation Street is one of the Queen's favourite programmes.

? Wherever she is in the world, the Queen drinks Malvern Water.

? You can only shake the Queen's hand if she offers her hand to you. At the same time, you should curtsey or bow.

? If you speak to the Queen, you should address her as "Your Majesty" the first time, and then you can call her "Ma'am" (say it like "marm").

? If you want to ask the Queen to tea at your house, you shouldn't really send the invitation direct to her. Instead, send it to her Private Secretary or one of the Ladies in Waiting.

? If you get invited to a party by the Queen, don't forget you can't leave until she has!

> *Extra Special Big thanks to Books For Students and their school bookshops*

More extra special thanks to

The Huddersfield Daily Examiner

Grimsby Evening Telegraph

West Lancashire Evening Gazzette

Bolton Evening News

and their readers.

Bloomsbury Children's Books would like to thank everyone who has helped us to compile this book. If you wrote your name down clearly, you'll find yourself listed here (and if you didn't, then don't blame us!):

A

The Abbey School, Suffolk
All Saints Church of England Primary School, Surrey
Charlotte ABBOTT, 8
Jenny ACKERMAN, 8
Mrs ADAMS
Daniel James ADAMS, 7
Albany Junior School
Almondbury High School, Huddersfield
Anand, 6
Lucy ARMES, 7
Bridget ASHBY, 7¾
Rachel ASHURST
Adam ASHLEY, 7½
Mrs ASHWORTH
Claire ASKEW, 9½
Chloe AUST, 10 ½
Nicole AZHAKESAN, 8

What does a cat say if you stand on it's tail? Meeouch!

B

Nicola BAKER, 8
Alison BALL, 10
Kristina BALL, 8
Rhiannon BALL, 9
Lucy Anne Margret BARBER, 8
Danielle BARLEY, 11
Katie BARKER, 6
Craig BARROW, 8

"Please save endangered species."
Christopher ?, 9, Sherborne Prep School

Christopher BARRY, 8
Ann-Marie BEARDMARE, 8½
Robert Michael BEBEE, 10
Carly BEDINGFELD, 8
Paul BENNETTA, 8
Stuart James BERRISFORD, 8
Tim BESLY, 9
Philippa BEVAN, 9
Hetal BHATT, 8½
Sandeep Ricky BILAN, 8
Gemma BIGBY, 7
Mrs BILINGHAM, 9
Claire BILLIAHD, 7
Michael James BINNS, 7½
Mr BIRCHALL
Mr BIRCHILL
Bishops Primary School, Newquay
Bolton Evening News
Books for Students

*What do you call
a sheep
without legs?
A cloud.*

Mrs BOOTH
Mrs BOYD
Jason BOYLAN, 7
Liam BRADEY, 10
Marie BRADSHAW, 8
Alice BRADY, 8
Jessica BRELSFORD, 8
Matthew BROWN, 7
Samantha BROWN, 8
Sally-Louise BROWN, 10
Robyn BUCKLE, 10
Jack BUCKNER, 9
Mrs BUCTON
John Martyn BULLEN, 11

> **❝** I think all the children would remember your 70th
> birthday if you gave everyone the day off school. **❞**
> Niall Scott-Helderdown, 8, Sherborne Prep School

Emma BURBRIDGE, 7
Jesica BURCHELL, 8
Kerry Ann BURGESS, 8
Mrs BURROWS
Jamie BUTT, 8
Mrs BUXTON

C

Rory CAHILL, 10
Calday Grange Grammar School, Wirral
Jamie CAPLE, 11
Alexander William Hamish CARROLL, 8
Sophie CARROLL, 9
Sian CARTER, 11
Steven Patris Remy CAVE, 8
Gemma CERASALE, 5
Laura CHAMPION, 10
Nanette A CHAPMAN, 8
Christopher, 6
Sophie CHECCHI, 5
Dahley CHAPLIN, 9
Stacey Ann CLARK, 8
Nicole L CLARE, 8
Julia V CLARKE, 7
Mrs CLUBB
Natalie COCKAYNE, 8
Mary COEN
Christopher COLE, 6
Thomas COLE, 6
Miss COLEMAN

What do you get if you pour hot water down a rabbit hole? Hot cross bunnies.

66 Tell Parliament not to have so many factories near fields because it causes too much pollution. **99**
Joshua Haddow, 7, St. George's C E First School, Kidderminster.

Isla CONWAY, 7
Mrs COOK
Richard Alan David COOK, 10
Daniel Ross COOPER, 8
Grace CORDERY, 11
Jaime L COUGHLAN, 10
Michael COUGHLAN, 8
Thomas Edward COURT DAVIES, 9
Tommy COWAN, 7
Deanna COWLISHAW, 9
Natalie COYNE
Jacob COZENS, 5
Crawshawbooth Church Primary School
Sam CUDDY, 10
Dame Alice Harper School, Bedford
Kyle DANKS, 10
Victoria Catherine DARCE, 10
Cecily DAVEY, 9
Jenny DAVEY, 8
Ben DAVIES, 10
Candice DAVIES, 10
Carolyn DAVIES, 10
Gwyn DAVIES, 6
Christina DAVIS, 9
Shane DAVIS, 7
Miss DAVISON
Adam DAVITT, 9
David DAWSON
Peter David DAWN, 8
Jordan Rose DE CLAIRE, 5
Jonathan DELCHAR, 10
Kerri DENMAN, 10

What bull sleeps?
A bulldozer.

> 66 Can you let the homeless people who are suffering
> live in one of your houses otherwise they will die of
> the cold winter. 99
> Jonathan Elliott, 8, St Georges C E First School,
> Kidderminster

George Patrick DEVER-CHAMP, 8
Nina DICKENSON, 10
Dominique, 6
Natalie DINNIGAN, 7
Mr DOBSON
Richard DODSLEY, 8
Timothy J H DORRELL, 10
Mark DRURY, 11
Mrs DUNCAN

E

Amy EBURY, 8
Stacey EDROS, 7
Adam ELLARD, 10
Sarah Louise ELLARD, 8
Ellen, 8
Jonathan ELLIOTT, 8
Matthew EMERY, 9
Lynette ENGEL, 8
Daniel David EVANS, 9
Jeremy Mark EVANS, 10
Joel James EVANS, 10
Lysia EVANS, 7½
Thomas EVANS, 6
Olivia ESAW, 8
Sohali ESMAILI, 10
Evenlode Primary School, Penarth
Charlotte EVERETT, 9

What is the crocodile's favourite game? Snap.

! 66Please stop drugs my dear Queen.99
Deanna Cowlishaw, 9, Ley Top First School, Bradford

F

Colin FAIRHURST, 9
Hywel FANNER, 7
David J FINDLAY, 7
Michael FLANAGAN, 10
Daniel Charles FLYNN, 6
Felicity FORBES, 8
Andrew FORD, 10
James FOUGHY, 8
Jon FOUNTAIN, 6
Michael FRAPE, 11
Emma FREEMAN, 8
Lauren FURZE, 7

TEACHER: Where does the Queen keep her loose change? REBECCA: In the Bank of England.

G

Katie G, 6
Lee GALLAGHER, 8
Sean GARDINER, 9
Daniel Thomas GIBBONS, 8
Mrs GIBSON
Emma Jane GOFFIN, 9
Miriam GOULD, 9
Mrs GOULDEN
Charles GORE, 7
Lucy GORE, 4
Kerry Louise GRAHAM, 9
Rory GRAVES, 7

❝I would like all the rubbish to be cleared up, please.❞
Elkie Louise Jennings, 9, Ley Top First School, Bradford

73

Melanie Sonja Yee GREEN, 6
Paul GREENSMITH, 8
Teleri GREGG, 11
Lisa GRIMES, 9
The Grimsby Evening Telegraph
Oliver GURNER, 8

H

Michael HADDEN, 7
Joshua HADDDOW, 7
Lillia HADJAN, 7
Stuart HAIGH, 8
Mrs HAMILTON
Natasha HAMILTON, 10
Rebecca Jane HANDS, 8
Sarah Ashly HANETINE, 7
Mrs HARDWICK
Michelle HARGREAVES, 7
Christopher HARROD, 8
Freddie HAYWARD, 6
Hugh HAYWARD, 6½
Rebecca HAYWOOD, 8
Mr HAZELL
Andrew HEARN, 7
Jamie HEARSON, 8
Zoe Claire HEBSON, 9
Mr HENDERSON
Lauren HICKS, 6
Amy Hannah HICKSON, 9
Mrs HILL

MISS: What do you get if you cross a queen with a ruler?
JUSTIN: A ruling queen.

❝People must stop dumping things in the sea.❞
Alistair Thorn, 8, Ley Top First School, Bradford

James HILTON, 8
Tom HOARE, 10
Ben HOBBS, 5½
Mark HODDER, 10
Caroline V HODGE
Matthew HODGSON, 6
Zara HOGG, 10
Robert William HOLLIS, 6
Scarlett HOWARTH, 7
Nicola HOY, 7
The Huddersfield Daily Examiner
Miss HUDSON
Jonathan HUGHES, 7
Clair HUISH, 8
Humbertson Comprehensive, Grimsby
Katherine HUTCHINGS, 7
Lauren HUTCHINSON, 7
Jonathan HYATT, 11

I

Tommu INWOOD, 10
Jennifer IRONSIDE, 9

*MISS: What do you get
if you drop butter
on the floor?
JENNIFER: Flora, Miss.*

J

Gordon JENNING, 7
Elkie Louise JENNINGS, 9
Fern JEREMY, 6

66 Something should be done about live animal
transport. **99**
! James Shell, 10, St Jude's C of E Primary School,
Portsmouth

The Jersey Evening Press
Alison JOHNSON, 8
Louise S JOHNSTON, 8
Mrs JONES
Catherine JONES
Charlotte JONES, 8½
Lisa Jane JONES, 9
Louis JONES, 4
Morgan Frances JONES, 10
Theodore JONES, 7½
Owen JONES, 10
Louise JORDAN, 9
Abigail JOYCE, 6
Camilla JOYCE, 4

What's the fastest cake in the world?
Scone!

K

Angeli KANUNGO, 8
Anam KHALID, 8
Mrs KING
Adam KING, 6
Samantha Louise KING, 9
King Edward's Junior School, Bath
Yasmin KOOMAR, 10

L

Anthony LACEY, 8
Mrs LAMBE
Laura LANCASTER, 7

❝Something should be done about the nuclear bomb testing.❞
Jonathan Savage, 11, St Jude's C of E Primary School, Portsmouth

Alexandra Sarah LATHAM, 6
Rebecca LAWRENCE, 10
Kelly LAWSON, 6
Cris Peter LEA, 9
Alexandra LEDGARD, 7
Kirsty LEEK, 9
Ley Top First School, Bradford
Justin LIM, 7
Carys Grace LLOYD DAVIES, 10
Lisa Ella LODES, 6
Kimberley Louise LODGE, 8 ¾
Jodie LONG, 8
Josh LONG, 10
Tom LONG, 8
Mrs LONGBRIDGE
Matthew James LONGFORD, 8
James LOW, 10

M

*What's the fastest fish
in the world?
A motor pike.*

Michelle MACDONALD, 11
Ross MACDONALD, 8
Thomas McCAUGHAN, 10
Wendy McCURRIE, 9
Christopher McKAUGHAM, 9
Oliver McFARLANE, 7
Michelle McFAWLD, 9
Luke McNAMEE, 7
Mr MAIN
Liam MANLEY, 6
Charlotte MANN, 9

! **"**Give the corgis a pat from me.**"**
Jamie Caple, 11, Bishops Primary School, Newquay

Serena Princess MANNING, 8
Natasha MANSFIELD, 6
Mrs MAPES
Casey Louise MARG, 7
Charles MARKLAND, 10
Yvette MARKS, 7
Mrs MARSHALL
Sally MARTIN, 9½
Abby MASTERS, 5
Hannah MEACHAM, 5
Matthew MEE, 10
Mrs MERCER
Pam MERCHANT, Books for Students
Middlethorpe Junior School, Grimsby
Callum MEREDITH, 4½
Jessica MILLER, 9
Moira House School, East Sussex
Jess MORGAN, 5
Nick MORGAN, 5
Vicky MORGAN, 10
Dawn MORRELL, 7
Lydia MOSSAHEKI, 9
Jack MUNN, 7
Oliver MUNN, 6
Scott MUNN, 10
Emily Jane MUMRY, 6

A man went into a shop and asked for some helicopter crisps. The shopkeeper said: "Sorry, we've only got plane"

N

Heena NAGJI, 9¾
Ian J NAPIER, 10

Gareth NEADLEY, 5
Andrew NEIGHBOURS, 8
Mark NELSON, 8
Christina NEVITSKY, 7
George NELSON, 8
Alexandra NEWMAN, 6
Miss NICHOLLS
David NICHOLLS, 9
Georgina NOEL-SHORE, 9
Sarah NUNN, 6

What does the Queen say to the Prince of Wales when he's naughty?
If you don't stop, I'll crown you.

O

Douglas OAKMAN, 10
Grant ORBAN, 6
Outlane Junior School, Huddersfield

P

Jay PALMER, 10½
Nicholas PANAYIS, 7
Samantha PARKINGTON, 9
Rebecca PARRY, 7
Natalie PARSONS, 8
Eleanor PEARCE, 7
Lesley PEAT, Books for Students
Penley Madras School, Clwyd
Mrs Penry-Williams
Anthony PEREGRINE, 7
Sophie PEREGRINE, 9

Philip, 8
Jade PICKUP, 6½
Jenny PIGOTT, 10
Camilla PIERRY, 7
Pinner Park Middle School
James Andrew POLLOCK, 7
Annelise POTTER, 8
Emma PRATT, 7
Natasha PRESCOTT, 7
Miss PRICE
Mrs PRICE
Matthew PRIDE, 7
Alison PROTHERO, 9
Elyn PUGH, 10
Owen PUGH, 8

*What does the Queen do in her boat?
She waves.*

Q

Charley QUINN-SMITH, 7

R

R L Hughes Church Primary School
Elizabeth RAE, 9
Alys RANDALL, 7½
Ramsey Spinning Infants' School, Cambridgshire
Naomi RAY-MAINUR
Mrs REAST
Andrea Louise REEVES, 7

Kimberly REEVES, 8
Miss REEVERS
Lee REYNOLDS, 7
Victoria REYNOLDS, 9
James RICHARDSON, 9
Susan RICHARDSON, 7
Nicola RIDER, 11
Victoria Louise RILEY, 7
James ROBERTS, 8
Mark ROBERTSON, 7
Mrs ROBINSON
Mr ROBERTS-WRAY
Matthew ROBINS, 10
Michael ROGERS, 9
Dean ROSE, 7
Rouge Bouillon School, Jersey

Where does the Queen have her Parties? In the House of Partyment.

S

St. Benet's School, Sunderland
St. George's First School, Kidderminster
St. Jude's Church of England School, Portsmouth
St. Nicholas' School, Blackpool
Mr SACKETT
Rachel Jennifer SALMON, 7
Sandcross School, Surrey
Miss SANDERS
Nisha SARIAH, 9
Jonathan SAVAGE, 11
Mrs SCOTT
Niall SCOTT-HENDERDOWN, 8

Emily SCHURR, 7
Sam SEDDON, 7
Patricia SEALY,
Fiona SETTLE, 7
Vicky SHALLCROSS, 9
Karen SHARPLES, 10
Gillian SHIELDS, 6
James SHELL, 10
Sherborne Preparatory School
Sarah SIMMONS, 6½
Miss SIMPSON
Mrs SIMPSON
Emma Cecilia SKIPPER, 8
Louis SMALE, 7½
Alan James SMIT
Mrs SMITH
Jessica SMITH, 8
Phillip SMITH, 7
Terry SOUTHAM, 8
Joseph SPENCE, 7
Louise Elizabeth SPENCER, 8
David SPOONER, 10
Mrs SPRAY
Alexandra STANBURY, 7
Mr STARSIKER
Mrs STEELE
Hannah STEIN, 9
Ryan STEVENSON, 8
Rachael STIRZAKER, 10
Matty STONE, 7
Ben STRARBUCK, 8
Jessica STROUD, 7½
Alastair SUDDABY, 6
Mrs SUMNER

When does the Queen know
she's been licked?
When she's on a stamp.

T

Emma TAIT, 7
Emma TATHAM, 7
Georgia TATTERSALL, 7
Douglas TAYLOR, 8
Laura Joanne TAYLOR, 8
Amy TENNANT, 7
Phillip Allan THOMAS, 10
Alistair THORN, 8
Christopher THURMOTT, 6
Suzanne THURMOTT, 8
Ruth TIERNAN, 7
Martin TRICKETT, 7
Thomas TROTH, 10
Niall TUCKER, 9
Oliver TUECKRE, 8
Daniel TURNER, 7
Emily TYRRELL, 9

*Why did the skeleton burp?
Because he didn't have the
guts to fart!!*

V

Hayley Jane VANDERSTOK, 8½

Rebecca WALDEN, 7
David WATERIDGE, 6
Flora WELLESLEY WESLEY, 7
James WHITTINGHAM, 8
Mrs WHYMARK
Ben WOODCOCK, 7
Mrs Wright